A.E. "Bean" Backus

The Backus School

Martin County Council for the Arts

Martin County Council for the Arts expresses its gratitude for the generosity of the Kiplinger Foundation for its sponsorship of this project. This program is sponsored in part by the State of Florida, Florida Department of State, Division of Cultural Affairs and the Florida Arts Council.

Contents
Martin County Council for the Arts
80 East Ocean Boulevard
Stuart, Florida 34994

First Edition

DESIGN BY RICHWORKS • PRINTED BY SOUTHEASTERN PRINTING CO. • STUART, FLORIDA

Contents

Foggy Sunrise in the Everglades

Preface

Every book should have a valid reason for its existence. This volume came into being as a result of hours of research and contact with family, friends and students of A. E. "Bean" Backus in order to define and document what has become known as "the Backus School."

As defined by the *Random House Dictionary of Art and Artists*, the term "school" is:

> *... a group of artists linked by a similar style.... Schools of artists have often been defined by geographical origin ... such as the British school or Italian school.... When the term is applied to a particular painter, for example "school of Raphael," this may either mean that the work in question was painted in Raphael's studio by one of his pupils or assistants (implying a degree of supervision by the master), or that it is a subsequent imitation or copy.... When the term is used in conjunction with a movement, for example "Impressionist school," it simply means (in this case) "the Impressionist."*

The purpose of this book is to verify Beanie Backus's valid and notable place in American and Florida art history, and to preserve in printed word and picture the progression of his style over his lifetime. That will give us the foundation we need in order to educate the general public to the Florida art history fact that A. E. Bean Backus was the founder, leader and inspiration of an art movement known as a "school." The book also records the people, places and things Bean felt moved to capture on canvas. And it presents the techniques, colors, work habits and art materials that he used.

The Backus School Exhibit, held February 4th through March 18th, 2000 by the Martin County Council for the Arts at the Court House Cultural Center, includes approximately 26 Backus students, some of whom started their studies with Bean in 1950. Though Bean taught for four decades, little has been done in the way of keeping track of the names and numbers of all his students and the degree to which he affected their art. Many of his students, individually, through the news media, have spoken of their affiliation with and affection for their teacher/mentor. However, to date, there has been nothing done to document the work of Bean and his students as a group.

It would be remiss not to mention Bean's influence on a group of black artists known as "the Highwaymen." Some of these artists did visit and converse with Bean at his studio, but they did not actually study with him. According to several undisputable sources, including Don Brown, Bean's last, long-time personal manager, his only known "Highwayman" student was the late Alfred Hair. In her article, "Florida's Highwaymen," published in *Florida Living*, May 1997, Ethel Yari tells us, "They [the Highwaymen] entered banks and loan offices, diners and supermarkets – and their objective was money." These artists were given permission by Bean to use his style and subject matter with the understanding that they would not sell their hastily painted, brightly colored landscapes in St. Lucie County. He kindly asked them to drive outside of the Ft. Pierce area so as to not offend his local art patrons. While credit can be given to these artists for seeing the obvious salability of Bean's artwork, they imitated Bean to make money. Yes, Bean influenced them, and, yes, they are a part of the Backus School – but they were not actual students. Most of the Highwaymen didn't learn from Bean, they copied him.

By no means was this project ever intended to be an all-inclusive documentation of Bean's life and illustrious art career. Most schools of art and their students are viewed from a much longer distance in time. The Backus School students have a few years to make a mark for themselves. Only time will tell us which individual students' works will endure and become noteworthy. As a group, however, they are well worth tracking, because there has been no other artist like A. E. Backus in the southeastern United States who had such a large number of students for so many years. In the art history of America and Florida, the students of the Backus School have no peers.

Sherrie Johnson

Guest Curator,

The Backus School

A.E. Backus and the Landscape Tradition

Albert Ernest Backus is one of the most renowned and admired of Florida's regional painters. He was known as "Bean" or "Beanie," in reference to the childhood nickname of "Beanpot" that was given to him by a family friend. The fact that he retained this *soubriquet* to the end of his days, and is still referred to in this familial way, is a reflection of the humility, accessibility and earthy humanity that characterized his life – a life devoted to art, friendship and, particularly, an appreciation of the beauty of his natural environment.

Although Backus did execute some portraits during his career, including an early watercolor likeness of his sister that demonstrated his precociousness, he is known for his poetic and atmospheric landscapes filled with light and color. These paintings capture a specific time and place, the place often located in or near his native Ft. Pierce, where he was inspired by Florida's flora, fauna and ocean views. His celebration of the tropical setting dates from the late 1920s until he died in 1990 with an unfinished canvas still on his easel. This last work (Plate XXVIII), as well as many others, is preserved in the A.E. "Bean" Backus Museum in Ft. Pierce, which was founded in 1961 and officially named for Backus after his death.

The life and career of A.E. Backus spans most of the twentieth century (1906-1990). Stylistically and aesthetically, however, his work is far removed from the abstract and formalistic concerns of most modern art. Instead, he recalls an earlier landscape tradition, which focused on naturalistic views of specific environmental regions, whether they be the olive trees of Italy, the forest at Barbizon or the Catskill Mountains of New York.

The beauty of the natural world has been capturing the imagination and fascination of artists for thousands of years.

Opposite: Plate I,
Ranch Road,
20″ x 24″,
Adams Ranch Collection, 1949

5

Pure landscapes (those without a figurative focus) date from as early as Roman times. They became especially popular, however, in the seventeenth century when artists such as Claude Lorrain (1600-1682) concentrated their attention on the light of the setting sun as it reflected off the Mediterranean Sea. This emphasis on capturing the light, shadows, mood and atmosphere of a certain time of day and specific geographical place would have a strong impact during the entire nineteenth century – a century when landscape painting dominated the art world. It was this century that produced Constable, Inness, Homer and Monet, all of whom appear to have influenced Backus.

The impressionistic approach of Claude Monet (1840-1926) is reflected in many of the landscapes painted by Backus, but particularly in his early works. In these paintings, Backus displays a bold spontaneity and impasto technique, which was achieved by applying paint directly onto the canvas with a palette knife instead of by mixing the colors on the palette and applying them with a brush. Backus approached landscapes such as *Ranch Road* (Plate I), *Light Breezes* (Plate II) and *Bream Fishing* (Plate III) with his characteristic *al prima* style – painting directly on the canvas without any underdrawing. There is an energy and brashness to these early works that render them the most original of his *oeuvre*. His calm and controlled later style, while serene and pleasing, is also more predictable.

It was, perhaps, Backus's exposure to the New York art scene while studying at the Parsons School that encouraged his early, more expressionistic style. He, himself, said that had he remained in New York he probably would have become an abstract painter. He did not, however, make that city his home. He returned to scenic Ft. Pierce, Florida, where he attracted the support and admiration of many patrons and students.

The Backus style throughout the 1940s and 1950s is characterized by a thick, rich build-up of paint applied in layers

Opposite: Plate II,
Light Breezes,
30″ x 40″,
F.A.U. Collection, n.d.

by a palette knife. During this time, he painted largely *en plein air* (directly outdoors), an approach first popularized by the Barbizon painter Charles Daubigny (1817-1878) and continued by the Impressionists, particularly Monet. As stressed by Monet, by painting on site, the artist was encouraged to capture only what he saw, not what he knew. *En plein air* paintings have a freshness and vitality to them that is not generally captured in more polished studio pieces. In Backus's *St. Lucie River Scene* (Plate IV) and *Orange Grove Road* (Plate V), for example, the viewer senses an immediate response to the scene depicted. Backus would later produce most of his works in the studio, based on memory and sketches done outdoors. This change is reflected in his paintings. His transitional style is seen in *Pine Woods* (Plate VI), which still employs bold colors and a thick surface, but begins to show a greater interest in detail.

The free, impressionistic style of Backus's early works would gradually evolve into a more detailed rendering that still concentrated on light and atmosphere. In these paintings, he recalls the work of Winslow Homer (1836-1910) in both style and subject matter. Like Homer, he painted many views of boats and the sea, with attention given to clouds and the elements that suggests the ever-present struggle of man vs. nature. His dramatic 1958 painting, *Boat, Beach and Storm* (Plate VII) shows a small boat precariously perched on the beach in front of a swelling tide and threatening sky. The tide is again the theme in *Storm on Ocean Beach* (Plate VIII), where the howling wind creates a rough and menacing sea. It is obvious when viewing these works that Backus keenly observed his subjects. In the case of boats and boating, this was not difficult for him, since his father had a boat-building business located on the water. The artist would eventually purchase this site and use it as a studio.

Of course, no painter of the tropics can resist the exotic beauty of palm trees blowing in the wind. This was true of

Opposite: Plate III,
Bream Fishing,
20″ x 24″,
F.A.U. Collection, n.d.

9

Boston-born Homer when he visited Key West, and it was true of Backus. Asymmetrical composition and a focus on the elements, particularly the wind and surf as it pounds against the palm-lined shore, may be seen in the works of both Homer and Backus. Examples by Backus include *Seaside Dunes* (Plate IX) and *Wind and Palms* (Plate X). Both of these works were once owned by Backus patron Thomas Fleming, who bequeathed his collection of 61 paintings to Florida Atlantic University. Other important Backus collectors include Dorothy Binney Palmer, Arthur DeYo (who sold his collection to Fleming), Arthur Vining Davis, Senator and Mrs. Bob Graham, Allen Morris, the SunTrust Bank and the Kiplinger family.

As might be predicted, seascapes are a staple of tropical landscape paintings. Of greater historic interest are the backwoods, salt marshes and inner creeks and rivers that were recorded by Backus while other artists remained focused on the coast. In works such as *E.M.S. Ranch Sunset* (Plate XI), Backus captures the sparse beauty of Florida's flat grasslands with their coexisting pines and palms, preserving for posterity a part of the landscape that is fast being threatened by the housing developments and population growth in this area of Florida. By recording the pre-urbanization landscape and environment of the region, he has done for Florida what the Hudson River Artists did a century before for New York. Two additional Backus works that project the isolated serenity of Florida's marshy terrain are *Late Afternoon* (Plate XII) and *Wiskey Creek* (Plate XIII). Only the birds inhabit his *Florida Hammock* (Plate XIV) and *Cypress Swamp* (Plate XV), giving us the eerie, nostalgic feeling that they will not be alone for long.

As the child of a pioneer family, Backus grew up in the settings which he captures so well with his brush. According to his biographer, Olive Dame Peterson, Backus was enthralled with all aspects of the vegetation he painted, and he was

Opposite: Plate IV,
St. Lucie River Scene,
20″ x 25″,
Adams Ranch Collection, 1950

very familiar with the plant and animal life of the area. He was particularly fascinated by clouds, which abound in his expansive skies. For artistic inspiration he looked to the seventeenth century Dutch painter Meinert Hobbema (1638-1709) and the nineteenth century American artist George Inness (1825-1894). Inness was a New York born artist who was influenced by the French Barbizon School. In *Lighter Pine Storm* (Plate XVI), Backus captures much of Inness's look and technique. The low horizon, clarity of light and atmosphere, and attention to clouds seen in *Pastel Afternoon* (Plate XVII) show more kinship to Hobbema, whose large-scale landscapes are considered some of the finest ever painted.

The more darkly lit romantic tone of the early Hudson River School are seen in Backus's Herons in the Glades (Plate XVIII) and *Lake Wyman* (Plate XIX), although one could never confuse the two locations. Whatever artistic influences he had, Backus was true to the look and feel of

his native Florida. It is for this reason that he is considered a Florida "native son." Backus has been honored by a governor and a president (his 1969 painting *Everglades National Park* was commissioned for the Lyndon B. Johnson Library in Austin, Texas), and he continues to attract collectors throughout the state of Florida and the entire country.

Since the Backus studio was in Ft. Pierce, it is only natural that he used the Indian and St. Lucie Rivers as a constant source of inspiration. This area has long been associated with the production of citrus. When Backus was a boy, it was home to many pineapple farmers, including his father. It was only after their pineapple crops failed that the family business became boat building. In *St. Lucie River Scene* (Plate XX), the river winds through the lush and mysterious forest of unpopulated banks along the river. The fertile ground of the Indian River area is represented in *Riverview* (Plate XXI) and *Poinciana Indian River* (Plate XXII). Both of these paintings focus on the red/orange color of a poinciana tree captured in the bold sunlight. Like the Impressionists, Backus concentrated on the light and shadows of a particular moment in time. This is demonstrated in his *Palms and Shadows* (Plate XXIII), a solidly composed yet freely painted work that accentuates the bold shadows created by the light as it hits a row of palm trees. An unusual element in this work is the inclusion of figures in the scenic composition. As shown by the paintings discussed above, most of Backus's Florida views are largely inhabited by birds and wildlife (if they are inhabited at all). This is not the case with the many works he painted in Jamaica.

Backus established a small studio in Jamaica in 1958. From that time on, the Jamaican landscape and people often served as his theme. In *Jamaican Dugout* (Plate XXIV), three men are hoisting their dugout canoe into a narrow river. Typical of Backus, he has captured the specific light and vegetation of the island locale. However, this work is more of

Opposite: Plate V,
Orange Grove Road,
30"x 36",
Kiplinger Collection, c. 1950s

13

a genre scene than a pure landscape, an approach he often used in his Jamaican works. Another example of this is *Jamaican Surfer* (Plate XXV), where islanders navigate a treacherous surf towards a cliff-lined shore. Backus said that the island was so populated that it was difficult to find a view without figures, a comment that was obviously not entirely accurate. It was probably his affinity for the Jamaican people, amongst whom he had many friends, that encouraged him to include them in his depictions of the island. He spent little time in Jamaica after 1970 when political problems caused unrest.

Backus said that he preferred the light at early morning or late afternoon, but some of his most arresting works depict landscapes in the moonlight. In *River Moonlight* (Plate XXVI), for example, the viewer is witness to the tranquility of the moon as it reflects off the water and palm trees of the Florida shore. In *Foggy Sunrise in the Everglades* (Plate XXVII), painted the year before he died, Backus best shows the influence of Monet, his hero. As seen in Monet's famous *Impression: Sunrise* (1872), the yellow of the rising sun in this painting is reflected in the water below, while the objects in the morning mist appear as dark silhouettes against the sky. Backus was eighty-three years old when he painted this most obvious homage to Monet. In a sense, this brings his work full circle – from the aggressively approached early landscapes with their bold build-up of color applied with a palette knife, through the more detailed and refined paintings of his middle years, and finally to the subtle stillness and simplicity of his late foggy sunrise. As with most artists, the mood of his works reflect the various stages and transitions of his life. He died where he had been born, amidst the still beautiful but fast changing environment of Florida's Indian River.

Backus was not an innovative artist stylistically. His work is rooted in the nineteenth century landscape tradition. He, himself, was quick to acknowledge that he eschewed the modernist style and wished instead to paint works that

Opposite: Plate VI,
Pine Woods,
25"x 30",
SunTrust Bank Collection,
c. 1950s

appealed to a wide range of people. He certainly accomplished his goal. He often had a four- or five-year waiting period for commissions, which he sought to fill by painting daily. His time was also devoted to teaching. Students flocked to his Ft. Pierce studio to learn how to capture the light, color and atmosphere that emanated from his works. Many of these students have forged professional careers as artists who, like their teacher, responded to their natural environment. Known as the Backus School, these painters continue to capture the tropical beauty of the Sunshine State. Through them, the Backus legacy continues.

Kathleen Russo, Ph.D.

Chair, Art Department,

Florida Atlantic University,

and Professor of Art History

Opposite: Plate VII,
Boat, Beach and Storm,
24″ x 36″,
Kiplinger Collection, 1958

Beanie: A Personal Portrait

"**S**herrie, your art is good and it's going to take you somewhere." Beanie said that to me while viewing the painting I had just finished in his studio. To this day, people visiting my studio continue to admire that painting – proving to me that Bean was right. His words now hang beside my easel and serve as an ongoing source of encouragement for me.

"I'd rather be known as a good humanitarian than the greatest artist in the world," Bean said the day before he died. And those of us who knew him remember him as both a humanitarian and an artist. He was a constant source of encouragement for an extraordinarily large group of artists. All three of his studio/residences provided personal, artistic and intellectual inspiration. Creative juices in the form of rum, turpentine and lively conversation were always flowing. These were places where artists were being nurtured, art was actively being created and jazz was loudly being played. If Bean were alive today, he would introduce himself and simply state that he was a painter who genuinely liked people.

Bean was a quiet genius. He understood and had the ability to contemplate and verbalize original thoughts. His dealings with other people were friendly, entertaining, diplomatic and always kind. Many people might call him a character. Books on art and literature, along with magazines like *The New Yorker* and *Vanity Fair* abounded in his studio and were available to anyone to borrow or keep if they so desired. His generosity is legend. While discussing charity, Bean used to say, "You have to give away $10.00 for $1.00 to work." All of his adult life and throughout his glorious career, he gave freely of his money, time, materials and food, and even offered a place to sleep if you needed it. Bean's students didn't pay for their

Opposite: Plate VIII,
Storm on Ocean Beach,
20″ x 24″,
SunTrust Bank Collection, n.d.

lessons. He shared, for free, his vast artistic knowledge with anyone who asked. He understood that even if you use his colors, subject matter, types of brushes and palette knives, eventually you will use them in your own personal way.

Who was Albert E. "Bean" Backus? *Mantle Fielding's Dictionary of American Painters, Sculptors and Engravers* refers to him as "an artist who dedicated his time to painting Florida landscapes. His painting *Everglades National Park* is part of the permanent collection of the Lyndon B. Johnson Presidential Library." In *Art in Florida 1564-1945* (Pineapple Press, 1999), Maybelle Mann says, "He was unique in that he was a native Floridian working as a painter. His focus was on landscapes in which color was used in a gentle fashion. We value these works because they show us a Florida that is fast disappearing, both stylistically and in actuality." And in *A Portrait of St. Lucie County, Florida* (1994), author Lucille Rieley Rights tells us, "Famous for scenes of the ocean's edge and Florida's Backwoods, native son and artist A.E. "Bean" Backus captured the true Florida feeling like no other."

I knew Bean as an art teacher, artist and close personal friend – and I write about him with great pleasure and pride. He had many friends, some of whom were notable writers. While at his vacation home in Jamaica, Bean often had dinner with Ian Fleming, creator of "James Bond." He was also friends with the authors Zora Neal Hurston, Marjorie Stoneman Douglas and Mrs. Jane Reno, columnist for the *Miami News* and mother of our nation's attorney general, Janet Reno.

Beanie's artwork is exquisite. Using a masterful technique that *looks* deceptively simple, he depicted the spectacular grandeur and brilliant sunlight of a natural, unspoiled Florida – leaving behind a historic visual record. His unique style is easily recognized, and was commercially very successful. Commercial success for beautiful fine art was also enjoyed by Claude Monet, John Singer Sargent, Winslow Homer and William Merritt Chase.

Opposite: Plate IX,
Seaside Dunes,
30"x35",
F.A.U. Collection, n.d.

The of owners of Beanie Backus paintings reads like "Who's Who." Former Florida Governor and Mrs. Bob Graham, former Florida Governors Leroy Collins, Dan McCarthy and Fuller Warren. Senators and congressmen, corporate C.E.O.s, newspaper editors, real estate tycoons, prosperous ranch owners, several Florida universities, large financial institutions, the rich and influential, and lucky friends. And that's just in the state of Florida. Bean had collectors all over the United States and Europe.

Bean Backus has an art gallery and museum named in his honor in Ft. Pierce, Florida, where he was born in 1906. He has his own festival, the Backus Daze Festival, which has been celebrated every spring since 1989 in Ft. Pierce. His biography was published in 1984. In 1993, he was inducted into the Florida Artists Hall of Fame in Tallahassee. The Backus School Exhibit and this book reach beyond all of these accolades to show the universal scope of Bean's influence – and the creation of the art phenomenon known as a "school."

Bean has at least 45 documented students, including some who studied with him as early as 1950 and those of us who will continue painting in the Bean tradition beyond the year 2000. His unique geographical locations, compositions, colors, techniques and subject matters – used by his actual students and countless other artists for the past five decades – add to the criteria necessary to elevate him to the proper place of honor he has earned and deserves: founder of the Backus School.

Sherrie Johnson,

Professional artist,

Backus student 1983-1990

Opposite: Plate X,
Wind and Palms,
24″x 36″,
F.A.U. Collection, n.d.

Plate XI,
E.M.S.
Ranch
Sunset,
22″ x 28″,
Riverside
National
Bank
Collection,
1984

Plate XII,
Late Afternoon,
25″ x 30″,
F.A.U.Collection,
n.d.

Plate XIII,
Wiskey Creek,
25″ x 30″,
F.A.U. Collection,
n.d.

26

Plate XIV,
*Florida
Hammock*,
20″x 24″,
Riverside
National Bank
Collection, 1960

27

Plate XV,
Cypress Swamp,
12″ x 16″, Riverside National
Bank Collection, 1984

28

Plate XVI,
Lighter Pine Storm,
25″ x 30″,
F.A.U. Collection,
n.d.

Plate XVII,
*Pastel
Afternoon,*
25″ x 30″,
F.A.U.
Collection,
n.d.

Plate XVIII,
Herons in the Glades,
25″ x 30″,
Adams Ranch
Collection, 1960

Some Painting Techniques of A.E. "Bean" Backus

Beanie's technique was just a part of how he made art. He was an artist who used paint to express himself. His wisdom, kindness, humility and philanthropy were apparent in his canvases. Understanding Beanie's work means understanding who Beanie was. One cannot speak of his technique without simultaneously speaking of the man. He enjoyed regularity, and went about any task with a sense of purpose. He chose foods that he could make quickly. He ate and shopped at the same places. He kept friends throughout his life and welcomed new ones. He was very much a contemporary, yet held old world values – and transcended both. He was an anomaly.

The following is an attempt to understand the man through his technique, in hopes that his giving may continue as it did during his life.

Beanie's Daily Schedule

4:30 a.m.: Beanie awoke and went to breakfast at Captain's Galley. Joining him for breakfast meant listening to fish tales, sarcastic verbal jabbering, and heated discussions on subjects like what the day's temperature was going to be. His breakfast companions were a strange fraternity of (mostly) men of all ages, fishermen and workers about to begin another day's work – a group that Hemingway might have described.

6:00 a.m.: Returning to his studio, He reclined on his chaise lounge and read his newspapers – the *Miami Herald* and what was then *The News Tribune*.

Opposite: Plate XIX,
Lake Wyman,
25"x 30",
F.A.U. Collection, n.d.

33

8:00 a.m.: Beanie started to paint in his neutral gray studio with a skylight accompanied by warm and cool florescent lights. He painted until noon, unless he was interrupted by visitors (who often came from all over the state and the globe). We "kids" would be around at various times. We didn't seem to bother him. In fact, he welcomed us with the lure of drinks and "goodies," as he called them.

11:30 a.m.: He counted heads and fixed lunch which, at most times, was a sandwich and soup with salad and a soft drink. Coke was his favorite because it mixed well with Bacardi.

1:00 p.m.: Beanie politely excused himself and retreated upstairs to take his nap.

2:30 p.m.: He came downstairs and continued to paint, taking a few breaks to read the newspaper in his chaise lounge.

5:30 p.m.: Beanie either fixed dinner or took us out to his favorite restaurant. After dinner, he went to his bedroom and slept with a fan creating a breeze at his balcony door.

2:00 a.m.: He awakened and read a novel or some magazines in bed, and then went back to sleep. TV was never part of his schedule until the last few years of his life. He acquainted himself with shows like "I Love Lucy," "Gilligan's Island" and other late night reruns that he had not seen in earlier years. He seemed to enjoy them more than he would admit.

4:30 a.m.: Beanie started his routine again.

Opposite: Plate XX,
St. Lucie River Scene,
25" x 30",
SunTrust Bank Collection, n.d.

Beanie's Canvas

Beanie opened up a can of soup just as he would pull out a canvas. He doctored the soup with ingredients just a he readied a canvas. Because he stretched canvases as he needed them, he bought rolls of primed cotton duck and worked

with sizes that were easily fitted in ready-made frames: 12″x16″, 16″x20″, 20″x24″, 24″x36″ and 36″x40″. He bought frames wholesale and had them available to put his paintings in.

When Beanie stretched his canvas, he first expanded the end of each stretcher strip by dipping it into water. He assembled the four stretchers together and used the corner of a door frame instead of a carpenter's square to keep the form square. He stretched the canvas from the middle of each side out to the edges, securing the canvas with a staple gun while using stretcher pliers to stretch it.

Beanie coated his canvas with an underpaint made of ultramarine blue oil paint and turpentine. With a darker blue underpaint, he made his preliminary drawing using a brush. He didn't use charcoal because it smeared and affected the paint that went on top. The painted underdrawing did not affect the top coat and could be wiped away if any alternation was needed.

He mixed his paint using a palette knife. When he needed to thin the paint, he dipped his palette knife or brush into a medium (made of one part stand oil, one part Damar varnish and three parts turpentine) and mixed it into the paint. He used retouch varnish spray after the paint had dried to enable him to see the color as it was when it was wet.

Beanie's Brushes

Opposite: Plate XXI,
Riverview,
25″x30″,
F.A.U. Collection, n.d.

Beanie used a palette knife and both new and worn brushes to paint – round hog's hair brushes of all sizes, as well as sable and flat brushes. He rarely used a square brush. For finish work or to create more detail, he used round sable brushes.

He made his brush cleaner out of a single-loaf bread pan and 1/4″ mesh. He placed the mesh from the top of the

bread pan on one side into the bottom of the bread pan on the other side and filled it halfway with mineral spirits. Over time, his brushes wore down, allowing him to create special effects in the making of his skies, trees, ground and highlights. If a brush was not worn enough, he simply used sandpaper to get it where he wanted it.

With his round bristle brushes, Bean created the soft edges found in his paintings. (He often stressed the importance of softening the edges.) He used these bristle brushes to make his palm fronds appear airy – or allow you to see through his cabbage palms, pines, oaks, cypress and coconut palms. He also used them to create texture. The bark on his pine trees, for example, looks as though it could be peeled off.

Beanie's Sky

Many artists paint the Florida landscape as if it were in a vacuum, void of any air and looking sterile and crispy clean. But, like Claude Monet, Beanie painted the light that changed so often, affected by the thickness or thinness of the air. And he painted the dirt that exists in nature. He always paid attention to weather conditions, because that's what he painted – and his understanding of his subject matter created a better painting. He was aware of the different types of clouds and the different times of day. If he had any question or doubt about what he was about to portray, he called a meteorologist at his local weather station to verify that such-and-such clouds went with such-and-such weather condition.

He painted the clouds first onto his blue underpainting. On a clear day, his blue sky is darker at the top than it is at the bottom. He made the blue dark sky on top by mixing white and ultramarine blue. He painted the lighter sky near the horizon line by mixing white and pthalo blue. For more dramatic afternoon and morning scenes, he added earth tones, reds

Opposite: Plate XXII,
Poinciana Indian River,
25"x30",
F.A.U. Collection, n.d.

39

and yellows into his paint mixture. He once said that if he wanted to make the clouds brighter, he would simply make the sky darker.

Beanie's Palm Trees

Though he always admired the way Winslow Homer painted them, palm trees were Beanie's signature. Using earth colors to mix his palm green, a kind of blue-green, he painted his palm trees both with brush and palette knife, loading up the knife for the highlight of a trunk, the heart of a palm or a shimmering leaf.

A palm tree's basic shape is a circle on a stick. The older the tree, the smaller the head and the thinner the trunk. "Watch out for landscaped trees," Beanie would say, "They lean only if they are competing for light with another tree." He taught us that coconut palms are the exception because they lean naturally. In general, palms do not lean in the middle of a space and they are not affected by other trees.

Beanie's Composition

Beanie heralded Dynamic Symmetry, also called "the Golden Mean," a system of composition that he learned while at the Parsons School in New York and rarely departed from. (The text he learned from and always referred to is the classic art reference book *Dynamic Symmetry, the Greek Vase* by Jay Hambridge, Yale University Press, 1920.) According to Dynamic Symmetry, if you superimpose a nautilus spiral design onto a rectangle, you will find the most dynamic point of a composition at the center of the spiral. To find the nautilus center, you draw a line dividing the rectangle in half,

Opposite: Plate XXIII,
Palms and Shadows,
24″ x 36″,
Kiplinger Collection, n.d.

and another line from one half to the corner, dividing the space into two triangles. You then crisscross another line from one corner of the whole triangle to the other, forming an uneven X with the two diagonal lines. The middle of the X is the center of the nautilus. All the other intersecting points are secondary to the center – and you arrange your composition accordingly.

Bean's compositions are very inviting, allowing the viewer to breath, inhale and exhale at a comfortable pace. Like the man, himself, his work is very accessible. He balanced the positive and negative spaces in his compositions just as he balanced the joys and difficulties of his life.

Repetition of Forms

There is a two-figured Caravaggio painting of Peter's denial of Christ. In his depiction of Peter, Caravaggio composed the hands to indicate Peter's gesture of surprise when he heard the accusation against him. The shape made by Peter's hands is not only at the most dynamic point of Caravaggio's canvas, it also subtly reveals the composition of the painting as a whole.

Like Caravaggio, Beanie repeated the forms in his compositions in order to make subtle connections. For example, he often repeated his cloud formations in his tree formations. To achieve the transcendent effect that Beanie sought, however, this eloquent technique had to be done on an almost intuitive level. If too obvious, it would be a distraction for the viewer.

Opposite: Plate XXIV,
Jamaican Dugout,
26"x30",
F.A.U. Collection, n.d.

43

Beanie's Last Unfinished Painting

It almost seems as if Beanie left this painting (Plate XXVIII) to show us his methodology. Here we have the quintessential Dynamic Symmetry composition.

As you can see in this painting, Beanie established his horizon line from the beginning with his blue wash underdrawing. He did this with a seasoned yardstick that he kept next to his easel. The numbers that you see on the bottom of the unfinished painting illustrate an old sign painter's technique that is used to enlarge a smaller piece and maintain the original proportions of the artist's original thumbnail sketch.

Beginning with the half-painted coconut palm at the front of the painting, imagine that Beanie had painted the last frond in order to complete the four o'clock position of the circle of fronds. The area of the yet-to-be-painted frond would then be the most dynamic point of the composition. He must have planned to incorporate that frond with the unpainted palm to its right.

From this point, move your eye in a spiral towards the left … through the heart of the palm … down the top ridge of the clouds … somewhere between the numbers 2 and 3 painted outside the picture plane … back up into the picture plane, perhaps at number 6 … and out at the top ridge of the upper right hand clouds. This spiral creates the major movement of the painting. Smaller movements are also at play here, and at times seem to challenge the major one. This is the kind of drama Bean set up in his work.

Opposite: Plate XXV,
Jamaican Surfer,
20"x24",
SunTrust Bank Collection, n.d.

Studio Artist?

A. E. Backus was a studio artist the way Albert Bierstadt was a studio artist. They both learned from nature, yet did a great deal of painting in their studios. Beanie had cataracts as a result of exposing himself to so much sun. Because of this, he curtailed many of his outdoor excursions toward the later part of his life – and constantly instructed us to wear sunglasses as much as possible. Even when working in his studio, he rarely used photographs. His later paintings were composed of the countless tropical scenes he had personally witnessed and committed to memory.

Michael Sitaras

Artist, Greek Orthodox priest,

friend of Beanie's since 1968

Opposite: Plate XXVI,
River Moonlight,
20″ x 24″,
F.A.U. Collection, n.d.

The Backus Colors

While in Giverny, France in the summer of 1998, I was looking over the catalog for application to the American School for Artists – and the list of required paint colors jumped out at me. All of them were the colors that Bean Backus used, the colors of Monet. He often spoke of Monet, admired him as one of the great Impressionists and often quoted him by saying, "Anything painted in the right light is beautiful."

Bean's colors, so like those of Monet, enable the viewer to actually see atmosphere. He painted early morning fog. He painted the prairie at midday. You can see the haze and almost feel the heat. A Backus painting of the backwoods in the late afternoon sun glows with golds and the warmest of greens. He mixed his oranges, reds and lavenders to perfection. Painting on location and witnessing the colors firsthand, some lasting for only a minute or two, was the teaching exercise he believed so strongly in. He observed the subtle changes as the sun dropped in the sky, and then put them on canvas while they were still fresh in his mind's eye. Moonlight in a Backus painting is so soft that when lights in the room are dimmed, the moon glows. The colors Bean used most frequently are:

ultramarine blue	pthalocyanine blue	cadmium red light	cadmium red medium
cadmium red deep	alizarine crimson	acra red	acra crimson
ivory black	cadmium yellow light	cadmium yellow medium	cadmium yellow deep
cadmium orange	raw sienna	burnt sienna	raw umber
burnt umber	pthalocyanine green	permalba white	

Opposite: Plate XXVII,
Foggy Sunrise in the Everglades,
16" x 20",
Sherrie Johnson Collection, 1989

His palette was a 1/4″ thick sheet of glass approximately 16″x20″. The underside of the glass palette was painted gray and the top was laid out as illustrated in Plate XXIX. He squeezed out his ready-made paint along the edge of the palette to make room for the colors he mixed with a palette knife in the middle.

Bean undercoated his paintings with a wash made of turpentine and either ultramarine blue or burnt sienna. The blue wash was used for most paintings; the sienna wash was used for sunsets or sunrises. After the wash dried, he applied his sketch by dipping his brush in turpentine and then in ultramarine blue or burnt sienna, depending on the time of day he was depicting.

The first month I painted with Bean, I stood with pad and pencil in hand, writing down the colors as he mixed his paint. It was impossible to gauge his measurements, because he painted the way many people cook (himself included). One day, after trying desperately to write down exactly what he was mixing, I finally asked, "Beanie how much raw sienna did you put in that?" His answer, "Oh painting is like cooking. You put in a little of this and a

little of that." He spoke with authority because he was a wonderful cook as well as a masterful artist. So like Monet.

Bean's use of color, cool against warm, make the stormy clouds in his paintings move. He used warm gray against cool gray. Starting with ivory black and permalba white, he added raw umber or burnt umber. The raw umber was used for the cool gray because it contains green, and the burnt umber was used for the warm gray because it contains red.

His morning and afternoon skies, known for their lovely pinks and lavenders, also had blues containing pthalo blue, ultramarine blue, white and a little burnt umber. Closer to the horizon, he used permalba white, pthalo blue and raw sienna. This combination, using the deeper blues closer to the zenith and the lighter blues closer to the horizon, gives his paintings a great deal of distance. The graying or bluing of the trees closer to the horizon line also creates distance and draws the viewer to the back of the painting.

In his midday skies, Bean used ultramarine blue, permalba white and raw umber. He noted that because the sun is high at midday, it causes light to reflect off the back of some clouds and onto the front of others. He accomplished this effect by mixing permalba white with raw sienna and a little cadmium orange. The very tops of his clouds are highlighted with permalba white and cadmium yellow light. Lavender made with ultramarine blue, cadmium red light and permalba white gives the contrast that makes the highlights stand out. Again, warm against cool.

Of all the colors Bean mixed, his moonlight colors fascinate me the most. His night sky is created with ultramarine blue, pthalo blue, varying amounts of ivory black, raw sienna and permalba white. The clouds are white and ivory black. He enjoyed painting an occult moon partially covered by clouds. To make the moon glow, he placed a small amount of white mixed with cadmium yellow light in its center. He used that same mixture on the edges of the clouds. When you look

Opposite: Plate XXVIII,
Bean's Unfinished Canvas,
30"x 40",
Backus Gallery, 1990

closely at his paintings of the full moon, you appreciate the effort he made to accurately represent the highlights and shadows created by moonlight.

Although Bean was an avid reader of all kinds of books, including art books, his knowledge of color did not come from reading. He spent years outside, painting, sketching and observing. Observation was a practice he preached. It was imperative, a must, to paint on location. In his words, "It recharges my batteries." In the latter part of his life, when he painted each day in his studio, the colors he used were not guessed at or created by trial-and-error. He knew they were accurate because he had spent over fifty years seeing those colors when he painted outdoors. He could draw on his memory bank because it was full of the colors of every time of day.

Bean helped so many of us see colors that we had never seen before. On one occasion, while painting in his studio, I asked how he made the sun reflect on the fronds of a cabbage palm and how he saw so many varying shades in that frond. He led me to the door, and pointing to the cabbage palm outside said, "See the color of that frond? The color of the light coming through that frond? And the color of the light bouncing off that frond?" In all honesty, I didn't see it at all. But after days of observing that same cabbage palm at the same time of day, I finally saw what he meant. He knew that observation is the only way one can really see true colors, just as sketching and painting outdoors is the only way one can paint an authentic landscape. It was an invaluable lesson that I'll never forget.

Bean's warm greens were created with pthalo green, burnt umber, burnt sienna, raw sienna, cadmium orange and cadmium yellow medium. Other colors that he used to get a warm green are yellow ochre and ivory black, or a mixture of ultramarine blue and cadmium orange light. The higher the value of the green, the greater the amount of sun hitting the frond. The brightest highlight (the "sparkle," as Bean called it) is a mixture of cadmium yellow light, pthalo green and permalba white. He cautioned never to use too much. He said that because a little is good, people believe more is better. Actually, the opposite is true. When applying highlights, he often left a small fleck of the highlight color. He reasoned that the fleck of paint would reflect light and make the highlight even brighter.

Bean created texture by shading from the dark side of a tree trunk to the side bright with sun, using alizarine crimson, burnt umber, burnt sienna, red and orange. He could also place a ripple, created by a breeze on the surface of a river or pond, by dragging a round bristle brush across the water with his sky color reflecting the zenith.

When painting shadows along the ground on the shaded side of a tree trunk, Bean made it possible for us to see into them. He always told us to remember that shadows move, but reflections (which he painted in a lower value) are stationary.

It took years and years of practice for Bean to know exactly how much of each color he needed in order to accomplish a particular effect. I speak from personal experience, for there are days when all I do is mix colors over and over again, using a little less of this and a little more of that. But not even now, do I feel that I – or any other artist – have fully learned how to mix the colors of the Florida landscape to capture its essence, its light and its life like Beanie Backus did.

Jackie Brice

Professional artist,

Backus student 1979-1990

Plate XXIX, Bean's Palette. The colors, beginning at the lower left corner and moving clockwise, are ultramarine blue, pthalo blue, cadmium yellow light, cadmium orange, cadmium red light, cadmium red medium, alizarine crimson, raw sienna, burnt sienna, burnt umber, raw umber, permalba white, ivory black, pthalo green.

A.E. "Bean" Backus Biography

1906.   January 3, born on Indian River Drive in St. Lucie County, Florida.

1923-24.   Left high school three months before graduation to earn money in order to attend Parsons School of Design, New York City, New York.

1931.   First solo exhibition sponsored by Dorothy Binney Palmer in Ft. Pierce, Florida.

1936.   Won Bemus Award in Palm Beach, Florida.

1938-39.   Won the Florida Federation of Art Best Painting of Florida Award, a statewide juried competition, in Deland, Florida.

1941.   Second solo exhibition sponsored by Mr. & Mrs. Don Blanding in Ft. Pierce, Florida.

1941-45.   Served in the United States Navy on the U.S.S. Hermitage. From the ship's deck, painted landscapes around the world, which were sold in a New York City gallery.

1948.   Set up his first painting studio on Moore's Creek in Ft. Pierce and began to teach adult students.

1950.   April 9, married Patricia (Patsy) Nell Hutchinson.

1952.   Third solo exhibition held at Fairchild Tropical Gardens Auditorium in Miami, Florida.

1952.   Began children's art classes every Saturday at the studio, a tradition that continued until the late 1980s.

1955.   October, Bean's beloved wife Patsy died.

1956-58.   Bean bought land and built his home and studio at Priestman's River in Jamaica.

1959-60.   Bean bought his home and studio on Avenue C and Second Street in Ft. Pierce, Florida.

1961.   Helped found the Ft. Pierce Arts League, Inc., a public gallery which he graciously authorized to be renamed the A.E. "Bean" Gallery after his death.

1968.   Solo exhibition held in Palm Beach at Whitehall Museum, home of Henry M. Flagler.

1968.   Solo exhibition, a thirty-year retrospective of Bean's work held in the lobby of the *Miami Herald* Building in Miami, Florida.

1969.   Commissioned to paint *Everglades National Park* for the Lyndon B. Johnson Presidential Library in Austin, Texas.

1970.   Solo exhibition of the Thomas F. Fleming, Jr. collection of Backus paintings held in the lobby of the *Florida Times Union* Building in Jacksonville, Florida. These paintings were given to Florida Atlantic University in 1976 by Mrs. Fleming after her husband's death.

1979.   Solo exhibition at the Governor's Office in Tallahassee, Florida.

1980.   Awarded the honorary degree of Doctor of Humane Letters by Florida Atlantic University in Boca Raton, Florida.

1980.   Solo exhibition, the Backus Retrospection Art Show, sponsored by the Ft. Pierce Arts League in Ft. Pierce, Florida.

1988.   January 15, Beanie Backus: Master and Mentor exhibition, featuring Bean and 19 of his students, held in the *Miami Herald* Building in Miami, Florida.

1989.   First annual Backus Daze Festival held in Ft. Pierce, Florida.

1990.   June 6, Bean died of heart failure in Ft. Pierce, Florida.

1993.   Inducted into the Florida Artists Hall of Fame at the state capital, Tallahassee, Florida.

1998.   Honored as Florida Artist of the Year by the Museum of Florida History in Tallahassee, Florida.

List of Students of A.E. "Bean" Backus

There is an unknown number of "lost" Backus students, especially from the 1950s and 1960s. Bean's death, and the lack of other resources, has left us with incomplete information about those he taught during those two decades. Martin County Council for the Arts Executive Director Nancy K. Turrell, along with Court House Cultural Center Associate Director Sharon Coffey and Sherrie Johnson, Guest Curator, worked together from March through December 1999, searching the state of Florida (and the Internet) in an effort to find as many Backus students as possible. They used state, regional and local newspapers and other publications – and contacted Bean's many friends, relatives and known students who, in turn, referred them to other students.

Paul Abstein	Paul Arsenault	Camille Arter	Tom Ashcraft
Mary Boggs	Jackie Brice	Nell Brimson	Don Brown
Juan Brown	Susan Campbell	Capt. Ray Chase	Mary Coulter
Wally Edwards	Mike Enns	Jerri Fisher	Richard Franks
Tommy Fresh	Judy Fuller	Alfred Hare	Danny Holt
Nadine Hoskins	Delores Hutcheson	Jim Hutchinson	Kevin Hutchinson
Dee Huxtable	Sherrie Johnson	Rick Kelley	Therese Knowles
Susan Mabie	Gertrude J. Myers	Vilma Norris	Page Ogden
Anna S. Paraskeva	Justina Pettit	David Race	Jack Roberts
Jacqueline Schindehette	Michael Sitaras	Rupert "Rob" Smith	Judith Strite-Campbell
Nora Summerline	Leslie Szakacs	Fred M. Turner	Tim Woods
Roger Zetren	Bruce Tomlin		

Index of Plates

Index of Plates (cont.)

Photographs by Tom Baumker, Peter Gorman and Robert Terry, Jr.